PARABLES:
STORIES JESUS TOLD

EZ LESSON PLAN

THE VISUAL BIBLE™

**A Study of the 17 Parables of Jesus
in the Gospel of Matthew**

Participant's Guide

Len Woods and Neil Wilson

Nelson
multi media group
A THOMAS NELSON COMPANY

A Thomas Nelson Company
www.thomasnelson.com

Parables: Stories Jesus Told Participant's Guide
EZ Lesson Plan
The Visual Bible

Copyright © 2002 by Thomas Nelson Publishers
P.O. Box 141000, Nashville, TN 37214

Scripture passages taken from:

The *New International Version®* of the Bible.
Copyright © 1974, 1979, 1984 by International Bible Society. All rights reserved. The *New International Version®* text edited for screenplay by permission of International Bible Society.

The Holy Bible, New King James Version (NKJV)
Copyright © 1979, 1980, 1982 by Thomas Nelson, Inc. Used by permission. All rights reserved.

The Holy Bible, New Century Version (NCV)
Copyright © 1987, 1988, 1991 by W Publishing, Dallas, Texas 75234. Used by permission.

All photos are taken from *Matthew*, featuring actor Bruce Marchiano (Jesus) and the photography of Robby Botha. These photos are used by permission and are copyright by Visual Bible International, Inc.

Produced with the assistance of the Livingstone Corporation. Contributors: Paige Drygas, Ashley Taylor, Linda Taylor, Neil Wilson.

ISBN number Visual Bible Stories Jesus Told Participant's Guide

CONTENTS

WELCOME AND INTRODUCTION FOR PARTICIPANTS

- When you open your Bible, does God speak to you?
- Can you remember the last time you heard the Scriptures read well in a public setting?
- How often have you been in a Bible study where the emphasis was on what the Bible actually said rather than on what people in the group thought?

Welcome to this EZ Lesson study of *The Visual Bible*.

When the apostle Paul wrote to his partner Timothy about the priorities of ministry, he gave his young apprentice the following instructions: "Until I come, *devote yourself to the public reading of Scripture,* to preaching and to teaching" (1 Timothy 4:13 NIV, emphasis added). If that short list of actions–public reading, preaching, and teaching–was meant to suggest time allotments, it would mean that a third of the time should be spent in the public reading of Scripture. That's probably not what Paul had in mind, but the fact is that in a world with few books and no printing press, the public reading of Scripture was a highlight of Christian gatherings.

Because their attention spans were not overwhelmed from every direction, believers in earlier times were better listeners. They didn't have computers, records, and CD burners to back up their memories, so their memories were alert, their senses were sharp, and they simply paid better attention to what they saw and heard. Compared to them, we need help. Our attention spans continue to shrink. *The Visual Bible* meets us not only where our media training has brought us, but it also takes us back into the Bible text. It can increase our concentration!

The Visual Bible reintroduces us to the panorama of God's Word. It opens to us the scenes of Scripture. It reemphasizes in a fresh way the importance of the context of specific statements in the Bible. "Reading" *The Visual Bible* gives us a broadened and deepened experience of Scripture.

At first, you may feel like you are missing a lot as you watch and listen. Don't get discouraged. Work on paying attention and using your open Bible to back up your attention span. You will gradually find yourself using the Bible less to see what you missed and more to confirm your recollection. Repeated use of *The Visual Bible* will greatly aid your efforts to memorize Scripture.

EZ Lesson *Visual Bible* Study Components

You will find the following components in each lesson, listed with their primary purpose:

- **Key Question for This Lesson**
- **Introduction**–Background information on the theme of the lesson.
- **To Get Started**–Warm-up questions for group interaction.
- **Watching the Word**–View *The Visual Bible* Scripture passages for the session.
- **First Impressions**–Review and record your immediate response to the Scripture passages.
- **Second Look**–Note, with the help of your Bible, the details of the passages.
- **Observations**–Reflect more deeply on the significance and the lessons of these passages.
- **Conclusions**–Bring the lessons from Scripture into your life by thoughtful application.
- **Choices**–Make decisions about your response to the lesson, and implement the applications you have discovered.
- **Roadside Conversations**–Brief, optional daily review studies related to the Bible passages in the lesson.

Other features include:

- **Sidebars**–Remarkable quotes and helpful definitions related to the lesson and highlighted within the lesson.
- **Host**–The role of the host is primarily twofold:
  1. to offer, not commentary, but context comments to prepare the viewer for the text; and
  2. to create a bridge over the gap between visual texts that we don't notice as much when we turn pages in our printed Bibles.
- **Scripture**–While the theme of the study may focus on a verse or statement within a larger text of the Bible, *The Visual Bible* portions have been selected to present a complete thought or scene within Scripture.

May you find your experience of *The Visual Bible* an igniting or re-igniting process that makes the study of God's Word a passion in your life.

EZ LESSONS
VISUAL BIBLE HOST
DR. DAVID JEREMIAH

The Role of the Host

In the EZ Lesson *Visual Bible* studies, the host helps to introduce the various passages of Scripture in each session. His role is not to "teach" the passages but to give some sense of the context, provide a bridge between video clips, and prepare the group for the discussion to follow. Again, the primary purpose of these studies is to expose people to God's Word in a way that will spur them on to further study.

About the Host

Nelson Multi Media Group is pleased to welcome Dr. David Jeremiah as host of *The Visual Bible* EZ Lessons, *Parables: Stories Jesus Told.* For those unfamiliar with Dr. Jeremiah's extensive writing, radio, television, and speaking ministry, the following will help introduce our host for this *Visual Bible* study.

Dr. David Jeremiah is senior pastor of Shadow Mountain Community Church in El Cajon, California. For ten years he served as president of Christian Heritage College in El Cajon. In 1998, he was appointed chancellor. Dr. Jeremiah is also the host of the national radio program *Turning Point.*

Having a wealth of pastoral experience, Dr. Jeremiah has served as a member of the pastoral staff at Haddon Heights Baptist Church in Haddon Heights, New Jersey. He was the founder of Blackhawk Baptist Church in Fort Wayne, Indiana, which grew from twelve families to thirteen hundred members in twelve years.

Along with his experience in the pastorate, Dr. Jeremiah has launched television and radio programs, including *The Bible Hour,* seen in five major markets in the Indiana area. *Turning Point,* a national daily radio program, is broadcast on more than one thousand stations. He was also the recipient of the Broadcaster of the Year Award for 2000 from the National Religious Broadcasters. Since 1996, Dr. Jeremiah has served on the board of directors for the National Religious Broadcasters.

Dr. Jeremiah is also a regular guest speaker at Moody Bible Institute's Pastors' Conference, Alumni Week, and Founder's Week. Dr. Jeremiah holds a Bachelor of Arts from Cedarville College, Cedarville, Ohio; a Master of Theology from Dallas Theological Seminary; and a Doctor of Divinity also from Cedarville.

He has coauthored, with Carole Carlson, two best-selling W books, *Escape the Coming Night* and *The Handwriting on the Wall,* which focus on the meaning of biblical prophecy. *Escape the Coming Night* was rereleased in 1998. *Jesus' Final Warning* (W, June 1999), nominated for the Gold Medallion Award, examines what Jesus told his followers about the end times. Other books include *Turning Toward Joy, Turning Toward Integrity, The Power of Encouragement*, and *Gifts from God.*

Following the best-selling *A Bend in the Road* (W, September 2000), Dr. Jeremiah has recently released his latest book, *Turning Points* (W Publishing Group, 2001).

Dr. Jeremiah and his wife, Donna, have four children: Janice, David Michael, Jennifer, and Daniel.

ABOUT *THE VISUAL BIBLE*

The Visual Bible, Gospel of Matthew, is a genuine version of part of God's Word. With the exception of the introduction to Matthew, every word of the "script" used by the actors comes directly from the New International Version of the Bible, one of the most widely used texts of Scripture in English. You will note that the chapter and verse numbers are provided in the lower right-hand corner of the screen, so you can easily follow along in your printed Bible text.

The objective of *The Visual Bible* is to eventually offer a highly creative, accurate, filmed version of the entire Bible. Several books have already been completed. They are having a definite impact on the way people experience God's Word.

You will probably find at least three big and refreshing differences between reading your Bible as a book and "reading" *The Visual Bible*.

The first is that when we read the printed page, our eyes lose track of the time that is passing in the story. We can read in less than a second a series of actions that may have taken hours or days. *The Visual Bible* forces us to change the pace of reading. When Jesus got into a boat, he didn't do it instantly. Jesus multiplied bread and fish in a flash, but feeding five thousand people actually took a little longer. You're about to feel and see that difference. *The Visual Bible* brings the Scripture to us in a way that reminds us that God's Word is not just words on a page, but God's story lived out in the experiences of women and men just like us.

The second difference about *The Visual Bible* is that it informs and corrects some of our mental pictures of events in Scripture. It fills our minds with background scenes from the Middle East and reminds us that Jesus lived in a crowded environment. There were people everywhere!

The third refreshing difference in Matthew's Gospel of *The Visual Bible* is the way that Bruce Marchiano, the actor who played Jesus, chose to present the Savior. You are about to spend time with an obviously joyful Jesus. Some people have a mental picture of Jesus that simply denies the possibility that he ever smiled. They seem to think that he would have failed, somehow, if he had ever laughed! They like to quote the shortest verse in the Bible—"Jesus wept" (John 11:35, NIV)—as if that's all he did. The fact that John made it a point to say that Jesus wept may also indicate that tears were actually an unusual response. Jesus didn't cry a lot. It is difficult to imagine that a somber and unsmiling Jesus would have attracted crowds and children the way he did! After using *The Visual Bible*, you may find your-self reading your printed Bible with the intention of thinking of Jesus smiling as often as possible.

One further note about the style of presentation that will help you sort out what you are seeing: *The Visual Bible, Gospel of Matthew* is presented in two parallel time frames. The old disciple Matthew, played by Richard Kiley, is dictating his Gospel to scribes or, on occa-sion, he is writing sections himself. At other times, we are actually watching what he is dictating. Be aware that the time frames can change abruptly. Sometimes Kiley's voice narrates what we see Jesus doing. Once this is understood, it actually helps us appreciate the way in which the Scriptures may have first been recorded.

If this is your introduction to *The Visual Bible*, enjoy this experiential version of God's Word. Allow yourself to witness what the original participants saw, heard, and felt as God prepared his message for the world.

THE MASTER TEACHER

Key Question for This Lesson:
What do the stories (that is, parables) of Jesus tell us about God and heaven?

introduction

Everybody can recall a favorite teacher or two. Perhaps Miss Gates, who gave you a passion for reading back in elementary school. Or Mr. Osborne, the Sunday school teacher who seemed to really care about your life. Or Mrs. Manning, who challenged you to dream big dreams and to think outside the lines.

What about "the greatest teacher of all time"? Certainly Jesus Christ would have to be the leading candidate for *that* award. The Gospels depict huge crowds of people flocking from all over to hear Jesus speak. Matthew, as much as any of the other Gospel writers, gives us insight into the ingenious teaching style of Jesus. Rather than dry lectures, Jesus used simple, often humorous, stories—called parables—utilizing common items and activities from everyday life to convey deep spiritual truths about God and heaven.

This workbook focuses on seventeen of Jesus' most famous parables. Because this unique study utilizes *The Visual Bible*, you'll get a real feel for what it was like for those first-century disciples to hear the master Teacher firsthand. Whether sitting on a hillside or walking along the road, imagine yourself an eyewitness (and "ear witness") to the eternal wisdom of Jesus.

It's likely that "video Bible study" is a new experience for you. If so, it will help you to know that the "scripts" of *The Visual Bible* video segments of your study are taken word-for-word from a Bible translation called the New International Version (NIV).

You can certainly follow the "video-text" with a different Bible translation, but it may be a little more difficult to follow the action on the screen. Before starting the video, it is suggested that you open your Bible to the passages covered in the video lesson so that you'll have the written text available for further study and discussion.

STORIES
JESUS
TOLD
Visual Bible Study

The parable was a common form of Jewish teaching, and the term is found some forty-five times in the Septuagint, the Greek Old Testament. The term is a compound word made up from the Greek verb that means "to throw, lay, or place," and the prefix meaning "alongside of." Thus, the idea is that of placing or laying something alongside of something else for the purpose of comparison. A spiritual truth would often be expressed by laying it alongside, so to speak, a physical example that could be easily understood. A common, observable object or practice was used to illustrate a subjective truth or principle. The known elucidated the unknown.

~John MacArthur[1]

To Get Started

Use these questions to focus your thoughts for the subject of this session.

• In your experience, what are some of the most effective and least effective teaching styles and tools? Why?

_____
_____
_____
_____
_____
_____
_____
_____
_____
_____

• When someone speaks of "the parables of Jesus," what sort of images or thoughts come into your mind?

_____
_____
_____
_____
_____
_____
_____
_____
_____
_____

• How many of the parables of Jesus can you list off the top of your head?

_____
_____
_____
_____
_____
_____
_____
_____
_____

Watching the Word
The Visual Bible Reading 1

Using the list below, locate and mark in your printed Bible the ten passages in Matthew 13 that you will experience in Reading 1 on the videotape. After doing so, view the lesson.

Passages included in this session:
- Matthew 13:1–9   Jesus tells the parable of the sower
- Matthew 13:10–17   Jesus explains why he teaches in parables
- Matthew 13:18–23   Jesus explains the parable of the sower
- Matthew 13:24–30   Jesus tells the parable of the wheat and the weeds
- Matthew 13:31–32   Jesus tells the parable of the mustard seed
- Matthew 13:33   Jesus tells the parable of the yeast
- Matthew 13:34–43   Jesus explains the parable of the weeds
- Matthew 13:44   Jesus tells the parable of the hidden treasure
- Matthew 13:45–46   Jesus tells the parable of the pearl of great price
- Matthew 13:47–50   Jesus tells the parable of the fishing net

> Jesus' stories are like wrapped gifts. The packaging of the story can either distract or capti-vate. But unless the package is opened, the gift itself remains unseen. Likewise unless one seeks the core of the parable—its truth and application—the lessons will remain hidden. Yet when discovered, these lessons prove extremely valuable. The testimony of millions of changed lives over two thousand years attests to this fact.
> ~ *The Nelson Study Bible*[2]

First Impressions

Our typical "learning" experience features impersonal classrooms with rows of chairs, marker boards, and nerve-racking, essay tests. Jesus enrolled his "students" in an altogether different kind of "school." Matthew doesn't feature every parable Jesus ever told, but his account does give us a good sense of Jesus' methodology. Make a mental (or better yet an actual) list of your impressions of the teaching style and curriculum of Jesus. Consider how you might fare in such a learning environment.

- How does the experience of watching and listening to the parables of Jesus differ from merely reading the parables to yourself?

_____
_____
_____
_____
_____
_____
_____
_____
_____
_____
_____
_____
_____
_____
_____

• Does this video portrayal of Jesus teaching his followers fit with your previous mental image of Jesus the master Teacher? Why or why not?

_____

_____

_____

_____

_____

_____

_____

_____

_____

_____

_____

> The religious leaders, whom Jesus called "hypocrites" and "nitpickers," followed Him to listen to Him. Not to learn from Him, but to gather evidence against Him.
>
> They thought they saw. They assumed they heard. They pretended to understand. But Jesus knew their wicked hearts, and He purposefully taught in such a way as to keep them from fully knowing the truth because they really didn't want to know it.
>
> Sometimes when we read Jesus' words, we think we see, hear, and understand, but we can't quite fully grasp what He's saying. But that's a different situation. He's not willfully withholding the truth from us. He yearns to share it with us when we're ready.
>
> Keep at it. Read His Word daily. And little by little, you will see, hear, and understand.
> ~Peter Wallace[3]

• The introduction to our video clarifies Matthew's purpose for writing his account of the life of the Christ: "I am writing this Gospel to show through the writings of the law, the prophets, and the songs, that Jesus of Nazareth is the long-awaited Messiah." How do the parables recorded by Matthew help accomplish this objective?

_____

_____

_____

_____

_____

_____

_____

_____

_____

_____

_____

_____

_____

_____

_____

_____

_____

Second Look

This is an "open book" study. Make sure you have a Bible open as you work through the following questions. You're not expected to remember everything. The Scriptures will help you keep track and correct what might still be unclear from the video experience.

- What parables did you hear Christ speak in this video segment?

_____
_____
_____
_____
_____
_____
_____
_____
_____
_____
_____
_____
_____
_____

- Why did Jesus focus attention on common, "ho-hum" items like seed and weeds, bread and fields?

_____
_____
_____
_____
_____
_____
_____
_____
_____
_____
_____
_____
_____
_____

- After the first parable, the disciples asked Christ, "Why do you speak to the people in parables?" How did Jesus answer?

_____
_____
_____
_____
_____
_____
_____
_____
_____
_____
_____
_____

• Does this reply from Jesus surprise you? Comfort you? Disturb you? Why?

_____

_____

_____

_____

_____

_____

_____

_____

_____

_____

_____

• Which of the parables in this chapter do you feel like you grasp better than the rest? Which parables still seem unclear to you?

_____

_____

_____

_____

_____

_____

_____

_____

_____

_____

_____

_____

Observations

Now that you have examined a bit about how Jesus used parables and why he favored this form of teaching, take a few moments to look at what Jesus was communicating about the kingdom of heaven.

• In what ways is the kingdom of heaven like seed? What truths about seed are found here?

_____

_____

_____

_____

_____

_____

_____

_____

_____

_____

_____

• What do you know about yeast, and what does this suggest about the kingdom of heaven?

_____
_____
_____
_____
_____
_____
_____
_____
_____
_____
_____
_____

• What is Jesus' point in comparing heaven to a treasure or a valuable pearl?

_____
_____
_____
_____
_____
_____
_____
_____
_____
_____
_____
_____
_____
_____
_____
_____

Conclusions

Note that the subject of "the kingdom" will be a recurring theme behind the discussion of all the parables in these lessons. The King of kings, Jesus Christ, came to reign … in individual hearts, over nations, and over all creation.

• What does it mean for the kingdom to be planted in people's hearts?

_____
_____
_____
_____
_____
_____
_____
_____
_____
_____
_____
_____

• What does it mean for the kingdom of heaven to grow and bear fruit?

_____
_____
_____
_____
_____
_____
_____
_____
_____
_____
_____

• How do Matthew's repeated references to Jesus Christ as a king offering a kingdom alter the way you think of Jesus in your daily life?

_____
_____
_____
_____
_____
_____
_____
_____
_____
_____
_____
_____

Since Matthew is concerned with setting forth Jesus as Messiah, the King of the Jews, an interest in the OT kingdom promises runs throughout this gospel. Matthew's signature phrase "the kingdom of heaven" occurs 32 times in this book (and nowhere else in all of Scripture).
~John MacArthur[4]

Matthew uses the word "heaven" as a euphemism for God's name.... Throughout the rest of Scripture, the kingdom is called "the kingdom of God." Both expressions refer to the sphere of God's dominion over those who belong to Him. The kingdom is now manifest in heaven's spiritual rule over the hearts of believers (Luke 17:21); and one day will be established in a literal earthly kingdom (Rev. 20:4–6).... In one sense the kingdom is a present reality, but in its fullest sense it awaits a yet-future fulfillment.
~John MacArthur[5]

The opening genealogy is designed to document Christ's credentials as Israel's king, and the rest of the book completes this theme. Matthew shows that Christ is the heir of the kingly line. He demonstrates that He is the fulfillment of dozens of OT prophecies regarding the king who would come. He offers evidence after evidence to establish Christ's kingly prerogative. All other historical and theological themes in the book revolve around this one.
~John MacArthur[6]

Choices

Even though these EZ Lessons will involve a survey approach to the miracles in Matthew, the Gospel has a penetrating effect on a person's life, even after a brief encounter. One of the powerful aspects of *The Visual Bible* can be seen in the way it allows us to experience the Gospel accounts much as the first witnesses experienced Christ's presence. They had to make choices based on what they knew about Jesus. They couldn't just walk away, because that itself was not a choice. The following questions will help you examine the choices you may need to make as this session closes.

• In what specific and practical ways have you seen your life altered by the reality of the kingly rule of Jesus?

_____

_____

_____

_____

_____

_____

_____

_____

_____

_____

_____

• What are some examples from your recent experience or areas in your life right now that need change in order that you might be a more attractive citizen of God's kingdom?

_____

_____

_____

_____

_____

_____

_____

_____

_____

_____

Roadside Conversations
DAILY REVIEW OF THE PARABLES FROM THIS LESSON

Daily Roadside Conversation 1
A "Dirty" Soul
READ: Matthew 13:1–9, 18–23
Reflect on this key question:
Which of the soils in Jesus' parable best pictures my current Christian experience?

_____

_____

_____

_____

_____

_____

_____

_____

_____

_____

_____

Resolve to have a heart that is open to not only hear the word of Christ, but also to let it take root and bear fruit to the glory of God.

Suggested prayer: Sower of eternal truth, keep me humble. Make me teachable. Cause me to be vigilant to guard and cultivate my spiritual condition so that I am always receptive to what you want to say to me and to what you want to do in and through me. Amen.

Daily Roadside Conversation 2
The Power of Stories
READ: Matthew 13:10–17
Reflect on this key question:
How much do I seem to be growing in my overall understanding of the truth of God's Word?

_____

_____

_____

_____

_____

_____

_____

_____

_____

_____

Resolve to have a heart that is teachable, that hungers for truth—even hard, life-altering truth.

Suggested prayer: Jesus, many who heard you during your time on earth turned a deaf ear to your teaching. Keep me from making the same foolish mistake. Give me ears that hear and eyes that see. Make me sensitive to your voice and open to the truths you want to teach me. Amen.

Daily Roadside Conversation 3
Christian Counterfeits
READ: Matthew 13:24–30
Reflect on this key question:
What are some ways "make-believers" try to pass themselves off as genuine believers in Jesus?

_____
_____
_____
_____
_____
_____
_____
_____
_____
_____
_____
_____
_____

Resolve to fight the common tendency in "religious"
circles to pretend (spiritually speaking) or to put on a pious front.

Suggested prayer: Lord, though silly humans can be easily tricked, you are never fooled. You look beyond mere appearances and see the true condition of the soul. Since even Christians can fall into the trap of "playing religious games" and focusing almost exclusively on external trivialities, I ask you to change me deeply within. I don't want to merely *look* spiritual. I want to have a deep passion for you. Amen.

Daily Roadside Conversation 4
The Power in Puny Things
READ: Matthew 13:31–32
Reflect on this key question:
In what ways have I embraced a worldly mind-set that measures success by size and prominence, quantity, and/or flashiness?

_____
_____
_____
_____
_____
_____
_____
_____
_____
_____
_____
_____
_____

Resolve to remember that God's ways are not our ways and that he accomplishes his best work using the most unlikely resources.

Suggested prayer: God of mustard seeds, you use little and contemptible things for great purposes. You choose the overlooked, the simple, and the despised to accomplish your grand spiritual plan for the world. Plant within me an appreciation for the "topsy-turvy" values of your kingdom. Amen.

Daily Roadside Conversation 5
Payday Someday

READ: Matthew 13:35–43
Reflect on this key question:
How often do I stop and ponder what eternity will be like for my non-Christian family members, friends, classmates, coworkers, or neighbors?

_____

_____

_____

_____

_____

_____

_____

_____

_____

_____

_____

Resolve to remember the sobering truth that unbelief has grave, eternal consequences.

Suggested prayer: Lord, your Word explicitly says that you take no delight in the death of unbelievers, that your desire is for all people to be saved and to come to a knowledge of the truth. And yet, many reject your overtures of love. Oh God, let this fact motivate me to pray more consistently and share my faith more compassionately. Amen.

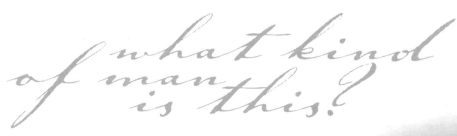

THE GIFT THAT KEEPS ON GIVING: GOD'S INDESCRIBABLE GIFT

Key Question for This Lesson:
What do the stories (that is, parables) of Jesus tell us about God's gracious gifts to us?

introduction

Gifts. We give them and we get them. For birthdays. At Christmas. On anniversaries. And sometimes for no reason at all.

Big or little, simple or extravagant, inexpensive or priceless—gifts vary so widely. But whether shared or received—gifts have the power to bring smiles to our faces or tears to our eyes. They can incite nostalgic looks at the past or spark hopeful thoughts about the future.

Our presents to one another can be wonderfully special, but no gift on earth—no matter how lavish—can compare to the gifts Jesus has brought his followers from heaven. Among the parables found in the Gospel of Matthew are four that give us a better glimpse of what the apostle Paul called God's "indescribable gift" (2 Corinthians 9:15, NIV).

What did Jesus mean when he told a story about a foolish man who built his house on a beach? What was the point of his account of a shepherd with a lost sheep? How does the odd anecdote about the generous wages paid late-arriving laborers help explain the amazing gift of eternal life? And the famous parable about servants given the challenge to invest their master's resources in his absence—what does that tell us about God and the spiritual kingdom to which we belong?

The answers in this lesson will startle and surprise you. But when we're done, you'll have a clearer understanding of the gift that keeps on giving . . . for all eternity.

STORIES
JESUS
TOLD
Visual Bible Study

One of my greatest anticipations is some glorious day being in a place where there will be no boasting, no name-dropping, no selfishness. Guess where it will be? Heaven. There will be no spiritual-sounding testimonies that call attention to somebody's supercolossal achievements. None of that! Everybody will have written across his or her life the word "grace."

"How did you get up here?"

"Grace!"

"What made it possible?"

"Grace."

What's your name?"

"Grace."

There will be more graces up there than any other name. Everywhere, Grace, Grace, *Grace!*

~ *Charles Swindoll*[7]

To Get Started

Use these questions to focus your thoughts for the subject of this session.

• In what ways is video Bible study (rather than looking solely at the written Scripture) changing the way you understand Jesus Christ?

_____

_____

_____

_____

_____

_____

_____

_____

_____

_____

_____

_____

_____

_____

• Now that you've had some time to reflect, what did you learn in Lesson 1 that has had an enduring impact on you?

_____

_____

_____

_____

_____

_____

_____

_____

_____

_____

_____

_____

Watching the Word
The Visual Bible Reading 2

Using the list below, locate and mark the four passages in Matthew that you will experience in Reading 2 on the videotape. After doing so, view the lesson.

Passages included in this session:

○ Matthew 7:24–27   Jesus tells the parable about the two builders
○ Matthew 18:12–14   Jesus tells the parable of the lost sheep
○ Matthew 20:1–16   Jesus tells the parable of the workers in the vineyard
○ Matthew 25:14–30   Jesus tells the parable of the talents

First Impressions

Maybe it's our sitcom TV culture, but we typically like stories with nice, neat endings. We want to see a minicrisis unfold and, twenty-five minutes later, have it resolved—all loose ends tied together, everyone smiling and hugging, and fading to the show's upbeat theme music. However, you've just watched Jesus tell a handful of stories containing certain confusing and even disturbing elements.

• If these four stories were shown to a national TV audience, which one(s) do you think would prove to be the most popular? Why?

_____

_____

_____

_____

_____

_____

_____

_____

_____

_____

_____

_____

_____

_____

_____

• Which of these parables brings you the most comfort?

_____

_____

_____

_____

_____

_____

_____

_____

_____

_____

_____

_____

_____

Sheep are mentioned more frequently than any other animal in the Bible—about 750 times. This is only natural since the Hebrew people were known early in their history as a race of wandering herdsmen. Even in the days of the kings, the simple shepherd's life seemed the ideal calling. The Bible makes many comparisons between the ways of sheep and human beings. In the New Testament the church is often compared to a sheepfold. . . . By nature, sheep are helpless creatures. They depend on shepherds to lead them to water and pasture, to fight off wild beasts, and to anoint their faces with oil when a snake nips them from the grass. Sheep are social animals that gather in flocks, but they tend to wander off and fall into a crevice or get caught in a thorn bush. Then the shepherd must leave the rest of his flock to search for the stray. Jesus used this familiar picture when He described a shepherd who left 99 sheep in the fold to search for one that had wandered off. The God of Israel revealed His nurturing nature by speaking of himself as a shepherd (Psalm 23). Jesus also described Himself as the Good Shepherd who takes care of His sheep (John 10:1–18).
~*Nelson's New Illustrated Bible Dictionary*[8]

- Which of these parables (in a nationwide poll) would cause the biggest uproar for its message? Why do you think so? Which one is the toughest for you to swallow? What is unsettling about it?

_____
_____
_____
_____
_____
_____
_____
_____
_____
_____
_____
_____
_____
_____
_____

Second Look

Now that you've pondered the overall impact of the parables, it's time to more closely inspect each one.

- What does the parable of the builders teach us about the kingdom of God given to us?

_____
_____
_____
_____
_____
_____
_____
_____
_____
_____
_____
_____
_____

• What does the parable of the lost sheep teach us about the kingdom of God given to us?

_____
_____
_____
_____
_____
_____
_____
_____
_____
_____
_____
_____
_____
_____

• What does the parable of the workers teach us about the kingdom of God given to us?

_____
_____
_____
_____
_____
_____
_____
_____
_____
_____
_____
_____
_____
_____

• What does the parable of the talents teach us about the kingdom of God given to us?

_____
_____
_____
_____
_____
_____
_____
_____
_____
_____
_____
_____

People are often astonished to hear that how good you are in life has nothing whatsoever to do with whether or not you go to heaven. . . . No one has ever been good enough to get into heaven if he did not trust in Jesus, and no one has ever been bad enough to be kept out of heaven if he did trust in Jesus. "Goodness" is not the standard by which a person gets into heaven. Rather, perfection is. If goodness were the standard, we could compare ourselves with others and perhaps squeak into heaven on our own credit. But, since perfection is the standard, we must compare ourselves with God, and when we do that, no one makes it.

Therefore, if we are to get into heaven, we must be made perfect. But how? God's perfection is credited to us when we believe in Jesus and commit our lives to Him. In that act of faith, we are crucified with Christ (Galatians 2:20) so that our old self dies in Him, and we are born again (John 3:7), recreated in Christ in holiness and righteousness (Ephesians 4:24). Why would God do that? Because He loves us. Out of His love, He gives us the gift of grace. No other gift is sufficient to save us.

~Max Anders[9]

Observations

The following two questions will move us to begin to crystallize and personalize the truths that we have been studying.

• In our day, society places great emphasis on messages being "user friendly" (that is, easy to understand and utilize) and on messengers being "tolerant" and "politically correct." In what ways do the four parables you've studied here fit or challenge these modern criteria?

_____

• What common theme or themes do you see in these four parables?

_____

Conclusions

After looking at all the facts and discussing all the data, there comes a point when we have to ask, "So what? What does it all mean?"

- Honestly, had you been present when Jesus first told these stories, how do you think you would have responded?

_____
_____
_____
_____
_____
_____
_____
_____
_____
_____
_____
_____
_____

- A friend says to you, "After all the ways I've messed up my life, God could never love me!" How would you respond based on what you've studied here in these parables?

_____
_____
_____
_____
_____
_____
_____
_____
_____
_____
_____
_____
_____

- You hear about a death-row inmate who now claims to be a believer in and follower of Jesus Christ. After a horrific spree of violent crime, this individual in an interview speaks of going to heaven. Can this be? Is it fair?

_____
_____
_____
_____
_____
_____
_____
_____
_____
_____
_____

> The word *grace* emphasizes at one and the same time the helpless poverty of man and the limitless kindness of God.
> ~*William Barclay*[10]

Choices

Someone has noted that "knowing what to do must be followed by doing what we know." The goal of the Christian life isn't information, but transformation. James 1:22 speaks of believers being "doers of the word" (NKJV). In other words, we must live out the truth we've studied.

• Describe the time in your life when "grace" became more than just a word to you—when you really understood that God offered you endless blessings, now and forever, as a free gift.

_____

_____

_____

_____

_____

_____

_____

_____

_____

_____

_____

_____

_____

_____

_____

_____

_____

_____

- What are some concrete and practical ways you can show those in your circle of influence the reality of the truth that the kingdom of heaven is a gift?

_____

_____

_____

_____

_____

_____

_____

_____

_____

_____

_____

_____

_____

_____

_____

_____

_____

_____

_____

_____

_____

_____

_____

_____

_____

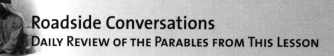

Roadside Conversations
DAILY REVIEW OF THE PARABLES FROM THIS LESSON

Daily Roadside Conversation 1
Solid Foundation

READ: Matthew 7:24–27
Reflect on this key question:
What are some real-life examples of people building upon a shaky spiritual foundation?

_____

_____

_____

_____

_____

_____

_____

_____

_____

_____

_____

_____

Resolve to rest your entire "God experience" on the gracious gift of salvation in Christ—and not on the defective foundation of human effort.

Suggested prayer: Father in heaven, thank you for Christ and for the eternal stability and security faith in him brings to my soul and my everyday life. Keep me from the foolish trap of trying to construct a "spiritual life" on anything other than your grace. Amen.

Daily Roadside Conversation 2
Searching Shepherd

READ: Matthew 18:12–14
Reflect on this key question:
When in your life have you felt like a helplessly lost, defenseless lamb? What happened?

_____

_____

_____

_____

_____

_____

_____

_____

_____

_____

_____

_____

Resolve to rejoice in the infinite love of a Savior who relentlessly seeks his beloved creatures—even when we foolishly wander from him.

Suggested prayer: Shepherd of heaven, thank you for your perfect mercy and your endless affection that will not let me go. Reproduce such compassion in me, so that I too have a heart for those who are hopeless and hurting. Amen.

Daily Roadside Conversation 3
A War Over Wages
READ: Matthew 20:1–16
Reflect on this key question:
Why is religion (the striving to earn God's approval and heavenly bliss) more popular worldwide than biblical Christianity (the teaching that salvation is a free gift that can never be earned)?

_____
_____
_____
_____
_____
_____
_____
_____
_____
_____
_____

Resolve to meditate on and marvel at the amazing grace of the gospel—we deserve nothing from God but punishment, yet in Christ we get nothing but absolute blessing.

Suggested prayer: Lord, your offer and plan of salvation defy human reason, drive out human pride, and destroy human notions of "fairness." Give me a deeper understanding of the gift of grace so that my heart is filled to overflowing with gratitude and joy. Amen.

Daily Roadside Conversation 4
Credentials
READ: Matthew 25:14–30
Reflect on this key question:
What unique experiences, abilities, material resources, relationships, spiritual gifts, platforms, and opportunities has God given me?

_____
_____
_____
_____
_____
_____
_____
_____
_____
_____
_____

Resolve to use all you've been given to serve God with all your heart and soul.

Suggested prayer: God, what do I have that I have not been given? Nothing! Every good and perfect gift in my life is from you. Make me grateful. Make me wise. Make me faithful with all that you have entrusted to me. In the name of Christ I pray. Amen.

Daily Roadside Conversation 5
Evaluation Day

READ: Matthew 25:14–30 and 2 Corinthians 5:10

Reflect on this key question:

If I suddenly found myself in eternity—standing face to face with Jesus Christ, having my life assessed— what would be my great joys and what would be my great regrets?

_____
_____
_____
_____
_____
_____
_____
_____
_____
_____
_____
_____
_____
_____
_____
_____
_____
_____

Resolve to live *this* day (today) with *that* day (the judgment seat of Christ) in view.

Suggested prayer: Jesus, as one who trusts in you, I know I do not have to fear the judgment of hell, but I do face a day when I will stand before you and give an account for my life. Help me to live in such a way that I hear you say, "Well done, good and faithful servant." Amen.

FINDERS KEEPERS

Key Question for This Lesson:

What do the stories (that is, parables) of Jesus help us discover about God and his infinite love for us?

introduction

If you're at all observant, you'll hear them fairly regularly—stories about wonderful, unexpected finds:

- the garage-sale shopper who bought an old, dusty painting for $25, only to learn that the canvas was a priceless work of art worth millions;
- the construction or demolition crew that unearthed items of great historical significance;
- the family members who were going through the estate of a recently deceased grandparent and discovered previously unknown collectibles—vintage baseball cards, glassware, letters from famous people, etc.;
- the researchers who stumbled upon a promising new treatment—and possibly a *cure*—for a dreaded disease.

We hear stories like that—or we watch programs like *Antique Roadshow*—and we sigh, "Oh, if only *I* could discover something precious and priceless! Why can't things like that happen to me?"

In Matthew 13, Jesus told four parables that illustrate this idea of discovery. These brief illustrations—almost passing comments,

some of them—highlight surprising truths about God and how, as Jesus tells it, his kingdom is something found, something precious, something wonderful.

Go into this session wide-eyed and with great expectation. Be especially alert and observant to the words of Jesus, just as you would be if you were granted the privilege of having a sneak preview of a spectacular estate sale. Those who seek, Christ promised, *will* find. And the things we discover will prove to be worth more than all the treasures this world contains.

STORIES
JESUS
TOLD
Visual Bible Study

> Many years ago, my wife and I visited the Grand Canyon with a younger relative of ours. He seemed curiously unmoved … while Margie and I gaped and drooled and mumbled in awe at the sight. Then, after leaving the Grand Canyon, we came upon a smaller canyon, much less impressive. I was ready to stifle a yawn, yet our younger relative was beside himself with awe. "I like this a lot better than the Grand Canyon," he said. "You can see it better." He said the Grand Canyon was so big, to him it looked fake, like a wall mural. This smaller canyon was small enough that his eyes could take it in.
>
> I think that is true about much of God's message in the Bible. His truths are so marvelous, it is hard for us to take them in. Our minds simply are not capable of grasping all the truth.
> ~Max Anders[11]

To Get Started

Use these questions to begin grappling with the subject of this session.

- If you could discover a priceless possession at an old rummage sale, what would be your "dream find" and why?

_____

_____

_____

_____

_____

_____

_____

_____

- What is the your most precious possession? Why?

_____

_____

_____

_____

_____

_____

_____

_____

_____

- Of all the truths you've learned from Jesus in this study so far, which ones have been the most valuable and helpful to you? Why?

_____

_____

_____

_____

_____

_____

_____

_____

Watching the Word
The Visual Bible Reading 3

Using the list below and a printed copy of the Gospel of Matthew, locate and mark the four passages that you will experience in Reading 3 on the videotape. After doing so, view the lesson.

Passages included in this session:
- Matthew 13:33   Jesus tells the parable about the yeast
- Matthew 13:44   Jesus tells the parable of the hidden treasure
- Matthew 13:45–46   Jesus tells the parable of the pearl merchant
- Matthew 13:47–50   Jesus tells the parable of the fishing net

First Impressions

We really should call this "Second Impressions." You've seen all this before. What jumped out at you this second time around? Did you see any little details or pick up any nuances you missed in your first viewing of this "reading"? Realize you have the luxury of a video that can be replayed over and over. You also have a written text that you can read and ponder—as many times as you'd like. Jesus' original audience didn't have these luxuries. Some of them only had one chance to hear these stories.

- How does the portrayal of Jesus in *The Visual Bible* differ from the way Jesus has been depicted in other filmed versions of the life of Christ?

_____

_____

_____

_____

_____

_____

_____

_____

_____

_____

_____

_____

_____

- How does your preacher or favorite Bible teacher communicate God's truth? How is his/her style like Jesus' style? How is it different?

_____

_____

_____

_____

_____

_____

_____

_____

_____

_____

_____

_____

TEACHING—the act of instructing students or imparting knowledge and information. As used in the New Testament, the concept of teaching usually means instruction in the faith. Thus, teaching is to be distinguished from preaching, or the proclamation of the gospel to the non-Christian world. Teaching in the Christian faith was validated by Jesus, who was called "Teacher" more than anything else.

Since sound instruction in the faith is essential to the spiritual growth of Christians and to the development of the church, the Bible contains numerous passages that deal with teaching (Matt. 4:23; Luke 4:14; Acts 13:1–3; Rom. 12:6–8; Gal. 6:6).

Special attention is directed to the danger of false teachings. Christians are warned to test those who pervert the true gospel (2 Tim. 3:1–7; 1 Pet. 2:1–3).

Sound teaching was a concept deeply engrained in the Jewish mind since Old Testament times. Moses and Aaron were considered teachers of God's commandments (Ex. 18:20). Parents were also directed to teach their children about God and His statutes (Deut. 4:9–10).

~Nelson's New Illustrated Bible Dictionary[12]

Second Look

Let's dig a little deeper. Refer to your written copy of Matthew 13, gather your notes from watching *The Visual Bible,* and tackle the following questions:

• See the sidebar quotes below. How do you interpret the parable of the yeast (leaven)?

_____

_____

_____

_____

_____

_____

_____

_____

_____

_____

_____

_____

_____

_____

_____

_____

_____

_____

Although leaven sometimes symbolizes evil, here the kingdom of heaven is being compared to the dynamic character of yeast. When yeast is kneaded into the dough, it expands by itself. Rather than being powered by outward armies or organizations, the kingdom of God will grow by an internal dynamic, the Holy Spirit, overcoming all opposition. ~ *The*
~Nelson Study Bible[13]

Leaven is almost always a symbol of evil in the Bible. In this parable the case would seem to be no different. The kingdom has evil hidden within which multiplies until it is found throughout the kingdom. The remarkable fact is that the kingdom still overcomes.
~W. A. Criswell[14]

• The parable of the hidden treasure is only one short verse. Go through that verse and circle the key words. Why do you think Jesus chose those words, and what is their significance?

_____

_____

_____

_____

_____

_____

_____

_____

_____

_____

_____

_____

• Scholars differ in their interpretation of the parable of the pearl merchant. Some say that *we* are the merchant and when God reveals spiritual truth to us, we should give up everything else in order to obtain the riches of God's kingdom. Others say that *God* is the merchant and that the point of the parable is to reveal how God looks for us and expends any price to have us for himself. Which do you think is the more accurate interpretation?

_____

_____

_____

_____

_____

_____

_____

_____

_____

_____

_____

_____

• What does the parable of the net help us discover about angels? About judgment?

_____

_____

_____

_____

_____

_____

_____

_____

_____

_____

_____

• What discovery is made in each of the parables in this lesson and what do these various "finds" represent?

Matthew 13:33 ————————————————————————————————
——

Matthew 13:44 ———————————————————————————————
——

Matthew 13:45–46 ————————————————————————————
——

Matthew 13:47–50 ————————————————————————————
——

Observations

Now that you have examined the parables more closely, let's begin to sort out all that we've heard Jesus say.

• Based on the four parables Jesus told here, what five adjectives would you use to describe God's kingdom?

——
——
——
——
——
——
——
——
——
——
——
——

• How do you think these characterizations of God's kingdom differed from the expectations of the disciples?

——
——
——
——
——
——
——
——
——
——
——
——

Conclusions

The problem with the truth claims of Jesus is that they give us only two options. Either we reject what he says as false and go on our way, or we regard his teachings as true and begin to live accordingly. Contrary to what many Christians seem to want to do, we cannot follow a third course of action: call Jesus' teachings true and then ignore them. That is hypocrisy. That is not a valid option for those who name the name of Christ

• What have you learned here about the kingdom's ability to spread?

_____
_____
_____
_____
_____
_____
_____
_____
_____

• Based on what we've studied here, how valuable should the kingdom be to us? How valuable are we to God?

_____
_____
_____
_____
_____
_____
_____
_____
_____
_____

• How would you explain the parable of the fishing net to a friend unfamiliar with the Bible and/or Christianity?

_____
_____
_____
_____
_____
_____
_____
_____

The salvation that comes through Christ may be described in three tenses: past, present, and future. When people believe in Christ, they are saved (Acts 16:31). But we are also in the process of being saved from the power of sin (Rom. 8:13; Phil. 2:12). Finally, we shall be saved from the very presence of sin (Rom. 13:11; Titus 2:12–13). God releases into our lives today the power of Christ's resurrection (Rom. 6:4) and allows us a foretaste of our future life as His children (2 Cor. 1:22; Eph. 1:14). Our experience of salvation will be complete when Christ returns (Heb. 9:28) and the kingdom of God is fully revealed (Matt. 13:41–43).

~Nelson's New Illustrated Bible Dictionary[15]

Choices

A Bible study like this is about more than, "What are you going to think or believe?" It's about, "What are you going to do? Will you follow Christ? Will you take him at his word and let his teachings change your life?"

Prayerfully ponder these questions, asking God to give you the grace and courage to take whatever action steps are necessary.

• What possessions, relationships, and dreams have you had a hard time "giving up" in your pursuit of Christ?

_____
_____
_____
_____
_____
_____
_____
_____
_____
_____
_____
_____
_____
_____
_____
_____

• Can you think of two people in your life with whom you'd like to share these kingdom discoveries—this week?

_____
_____
_____
_____
_____
_____
_____
_____
_____
_____
_____
_____
_____
_____
_____
_____
_____

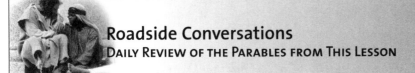

Roadside Conversations
DAILY REVIEW OF THE PARABLES FROM THIS LESSON

Daily Roadside Conversation 1
Influence

READ: Matthew 13:33
Reflect on this key question:
Which is truer of me—that worldly values permeate and dominate my life or that I influence those around me by faithfully living out God's eternal values?

_____

_____

_____

_____

_____

_____

_____

_____

_____

_____

_____

_____

Resolve to make a difference in your sphere of influence by sharing the love of Christ and shining the light of Christ.

Suggested prayer: I want to have a positive impact, Lord, on those around me today. Give me your power and wisdom to know how to be a change agent in the relationships and situations in which I find myself. Amen.

Daily Roadside Conversation 2
Valuables!

READ: Matthew 13:44
Reflect on this key question:
If an unknown observer followed you around for a week, what would he/she say you value above all else?

_____

_____

_____

_____

_____

_____

_____

_____

_____

_____

_____

_____

Resolve to reflect upon the fading, temporal value of the things of earth and the eternal treasure that is Christ and his kingdom.

Suggested prayer: Lord, forgive me for the times I treat mundane things as having ultimate worth and ultimate treasures as being of little value. Renew my mind. Grant me the grace to see both this world and the world to come with your eyes. Wherever my treasure is, there will my heart be also. Amen.

Daily Roadside Conversation 3
Bought!
READ: Matthew 13:45–46
Reflect on this key question:
How often do I stop and consider that Christ has purchased me, that I belong to him, and that he, therefore, has the right to direct my life?

_____

_____

_____

_____

_____

_____

_____

_____

_____

_____

_____

_____

_____

Resolve to live this day mindful of the fact that you are both precious to God and obliged by God to live as he commands.

Suggested prayer: Father, I am not my own. I've been bought with a price. Thank you for loving me enough to seek and save me. Remind me this day to live for your purposes and not my own. Amen.

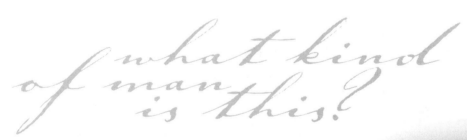

what kind of man is this?

Daily Roadside Conversation 4
The Great Catch

READ: Matthew 13:47–50
Reflect on this key question:
How earnest am I in being a "fisher of men"—one who "catches" others for God?

_____
_____
_____
_____
_____
_____
_____
_____
_____
_____
_____
_____
_____

Resolve to be diligent in casting the net of the gospel over your sphere of influence so that others have a chance to hear about Christ and his love.

Suggested prayer: Jesus, it is not my responsibility to judge people or to assess how spiritual they are. You simply call me to follow you and be a fisher of men (Matthew 4:19). Give me the courage and strength to speak your truth in love to those with whom I come in contact today.

Daily Roadside Conversation 5
Storehouse

READ: Matthew 13:52
Reflect on this key question:
How diligent am I when it comes to storing up God's truth in my heart? Or put another way, how much of what God has said can I summon from memory?

_____
_____
_____
_____
_____
_____
_____
_____
_____
_____
_____
_____

Resolve to hide God's Word in your heart so that you might not sin against God and so that you might have the weapon of truth to use in fighting against the lies of the evil one.

Suggested prayer: God, keep me from the common thought that the Bible is a helpful reference book. Impress upon me the truth that your Word is truth, and that I change in direct relation to how much I fill my heart and soul with Scripture, and how much I let it renew my mind. Amen.

THY KINGDOM COME!

Key Question for This Lesson:
What do the stories (that is, parables) of Jesus help us discover about the ultimate arrival of the kingdom of heaven?

introduction

Everybody has deep hopes and dreams. You close your eyes and picture . . . what? A long life filled with health and happiness? A satisfying, joy-filled marriage? Children who grow up to love and serve God and others? A big home? A thriving business or fulfilling career? A circle of close, lifelong friends? What's your dream?

Some positive thinkers tell us that believing is the first step toward seeing our hopes become reality. They assure us that we have the power within ourselves to make all our dreams come true. Faith + hard work = success. Guaranteed. Automatic.

And yet, as nice as that sounds, life doesn't always work that way. Millions of people—no matter how much they believe, no matter how tirelessly they try—go their whole lives and never see their deep longings materialize. Unexpected obstacles and unforeseen events, one after another, keep them from realizing their dreams.

If all this sounds depressing, it is not meant to be so. The world disappoints; God doesn't. There is one hope that absolutely cannot be thwarted—the coming of God's kingdom into this world. This kingdom dawned when Jesus Christ appeared in human history two millennia ago. He taught his followers to pray "your kingdom come" (Matthew 6:10 NIV). And the Scriptures reveal—especially the parables we will look at in this lesson—that God will answer this prayer. The kingdom of heaven *will* come in all its fullness at a specific point in the future—a time known only to God.

When that day arrives, the whole world will acknowledge the kingship of Jesus. And they will say with the psalmist: "Clap your hands, all you people. Shout to God with joy. The LORD Most High is wonderful. He is the great King over all the earth!" (Psalm 47:1–2, NCV).

STORIES
JESUS
TOLD
Visual Bible Study

Hope deferred makes the heart sick, but a longing fulfilled is a tree of life. (Proverbs 13:12, NIV).]

The creation waits in eager expectation for the sons of God to be revealed. For the creation was subjected to frustration, not by its own choice, but by the will of the one who subjected it, in hope that the creation itself will be liberated from its bondage to decay and brought into the glorious freedom of the children of God. We know that the whole creation has been groaning as in the pains of childbirth right up to the present time. Not only so, but we ourselves, who have the firstfruits of the Spirit, groan inwardly as we wait eagerly for our adoption as sons, the redemption of our bodies. For in this hope we were saved. But hope that is seen is no hope at all. Who hopes for what he already has? But if we hope for what we do not yet have, we wait for it patiently. (Romans 8:19–25, NIV)

To Get Started

Use these questions to focus your thoughts for the subject of this session.

• Describe a dream of yours that has come true. How about one that is yet to be realized?

_____

_____

_____

_____

_____

_____

_____

_____

_____

_____

_____

_____

_____

_____

• What is the most surprising thing you've learned thus far about the kingdom of God?

_____

_____

_____

_____

_____

_____

_____

_____

_____

_____

_____

_____

Watching the Word
The Visual Bible Reading 4

Using the list below and a Bible (or a photocopy of this lesson's text from Matthew—if provided by your leader), locate and mark the six parables in Matthew that you will experience in Reading 4 on the videotape. After doing so, view the lesson together.

Passages included in this session:
- Matthew 18:23–35   Jesus tells the parable of the unmerciful servant
- Matthew 21:28–32   Jesus tells the parable of the two sons
- Matthew 21:33–45   Jesus tells the parable of the tenants
- Matthew 22:2–14   Jesus tells the parable of the marriage of the king's son
- Matthew 24:32–34   Jesus tells the parable of the fig tree
- Matthew 25:1–13   Jesus tells the parable of the ten virgins

First Impressions

There's an old saying among teachers that goes like this: "I hear, I forget; I see, I remember; I do, I understand." The idea here is that lecturing is probably the worst way to impart truth, while involving students in the learning process is the best way to get them to grasp the material being taught.

• How did Jesus use humor, emotion, boldness, and audience participation to get his message across?

_____
_____
_____
_____
_____
_____
_____
_____
_____
_____
_____
_____
_____
_____

• How does this *Visual Bible* portrayal of Jesus acting out parables with his followers change the way you've always imagined these Bible scenes and stories?

_____
_____
_____
_____
_____
_____
_____
_____
_____
_____
_____
_____
_____
_____

• Do you think Jesus had a good sense of humor? Why or why not?

_____

_____

_____

_____

_____

_____

_____

_____

_____

_____

_____

_____

_____

> I would have less wish to go to heaven if I knew that God would not understand a joke.
> —Martin Luther
>   It is the soul that is not yet sure of its God that is afraid to laugh in His presence.
> —George MacDonald
>   The Bible speaks of a time when all tears shall be wiped away. But it makes no mention
> of a time when we shall cease to smile. —J. D. Eppinga
> *Inspiring Quotations Contemporary and Classical*[16]

Second Look

Armed with your video recollections, personal notes, and Bible text open in front of you, let's more closely examine the parables we just heard Jesus teach.

• What is the issue under discussion in the parable of the unmerciful servant (Matthew 18:23–35)?

_____

_____

_____

_____

_____

_____

_____

_____

_____

_____

_____

_____

_____

• What was Jesus communicating in the parable of the two sons (Matthew 21:28–32)?

_____

_____

_____

_____

_____

_____

_____

_____

_____

_____

_____

_____

• How did the parable of the tenants act as a kind of prophecy (Matthew 21:33–45)?

_____

_____

_____

_____

_____

_____

_____

_____

_____

_____

_____

_____

• How does the parable of the marriage of the king's son echo and amplify the message of the parable of the tenants (Matthew 22:2–14)?

_____

_____

_____

_____

_____

_____

_____

_____

_____

_____

_____

_____

• What does Jesus' parable of the fig tree tell us about the final arrival of God's kingdom (Matthew 24:32–34)?

_____
_____
_____
_____
_____
_____
_____
_____
_____
_____
_____

• In what way is the parable of the ten virgins a warning (Matthew 25:1–13)?

_____
_____
_____
_____
_____
_____
_____
_____
_____
_____
_____
_____
_____

Observations

Now that you have examined these parables in greater depth, reflect on the way the Matthew described (and *The Visual Bible* portrayed) these scenes.

• What do you notice about Jesus as he told these stories? What was his tone or mood in each situation? Why?

_____
_____
_____
_____
_____
_____
_____
_____
_____
_____
_____
_____

• As you watched the video "readings," what assorted responses did you detect among Christ's audience?

_____

_____

_____

_____

_____

_____

_____

_____

_____

_____

_____

_____

_____

Conclusions

In our study of the parables of Jesus in the Gospel of Matthew, we've learned much about the kingdom of God or kingdom of heaven, as Matthew seemed to prefer to call it. We've examined parables that deal with the kingdom *planted*, others that focus on the kingdom *given*, still others that focus on the kingdom *found*, and we conclude here with parables (promises, really) of the kingdom *fulfilled.* Use the following questions to take these various strands of truth and weave them into a beautiful tapestry of hope realized.

• What conclusions can we draw from Jesus' stories here about when exactly the kingdom will be fulfilled?

_____

_____

_____

_____

_____

_____

_____

_____

_____

_____

_____

_____

• Does it concern you that the most violent opponents to Christ and his kingdom were religious people? What does this imply?

_____

_____

_____

_____

_____

_____

_____

_____

_____

_____

• Based on everything you've studied in these four lessons, what kind of person gets to experience the wonder and joy of God's kingdom?

_____

_____

_____

_____

_____

_____

_____

_____

_____

_____

_____

_____

_____

_____

_____

_____

Choices

Someone has wisely observed that God didn't give us the Bible to make us smarter sinners. Rather he gave us his Word to make us holier saints. Put another way, it's not a question of how much we get into the Scripture. The real issue is how much the Scripture gets into us—changing our attitudes, values, and ultimately our actions.

• What one truth has hit you hardest in today's lesson, and what specifically do you intend to do about it?

_____

_____

_____

_____

_____

_____

_____

_____

_____

_____

_____

_____

_____

_____

_____

KINGDOM OF GOD, KINGDOM OF HEAVEN – God's rule of grace in the world, a future period foretold by the prophets of the Old Testament and identified by Jesus as beginning with His public ministry. The kingdom of God is the experience of blessedness, like that of the Garden of Eden, where evil is fully overcome and where those who live in the kingdom know only happiness, peace, and joy. This was the main expectation of the Old Testament prophets about the future.

John the Baptist astonished his hearers when he announced that this expected and hoped-for kingdom was "at hand" in the person of Jesus (Matt. 3:2). Jesus repeated this message (Matt. 4:17; Mark 1:15), but He went even further by announcing clearly that the kingdom was already present in His ministry: "If I cast out demons by the Spirit of God, surely the kingdom of God has come upon you" (Matt. 12:28). Jesus was the full embodiment of the kingdom.

The entire ministry of Jesus is understood in relation to this important declaration of the presence of the kingdom. His ethical teachings, for example, cannot be understood apart from the announcement of the kingdom. They are ethics of the kingdom; the perfection to which they point makes no sense apart from the present experience of the kingdom. Participation in the new reality of the kingdom involves a follower of Jesus in a call to the highest righteousness (Matt. 5:20).

The acts and deeds of Jesus likewise make sense only in the larger context of proclaiming the kingdom. When John the Baptist asked whether Jesus was "the Coming One," or the Messiah, Jesus answered by recounting some of His deeds of healing (Matt. 11:5). The reference in these words to the expectation of a MESSIAH, especially of the prophet Isaiah (Is. 29:18–19; 35:5–6; 61:1), could not have been missed by John. At the synagogue in Nazareth, Jesus read a passage from Isaiah 61 about the coming messianic age and then made the astonishing announcement, "Today this Scripture is fulfilled in your hearing" (Luke 4:21).

All that Jesus did is related to this claim that the kingdom of God has dawned through His ministry. His healings were manifestations of the presence of the kingdom. In these deeds there was a direct confrontation between God and the forces of evil, or Satan and his demons. Summarizing His ministry, Jesus declared, "I saw Satan fall like lightning from heaven" (Luke 10:18). Satan and evil are in retreat now that the kingdom has made its entrance into human history. This is an anticipation of the final age of perfection that will be realized at Christ's return.

Although the gospels of Matthew, Mark, Luke, and John focus on the present aspect of the kingdom of God, it is also clear that the kingdom will be realized perfectly only at the SECOND COMING. The kingdom that comes through the ministry of Jesus dawns in the form of a mystery. Although it is physically present in the deeds and words of Jesus, it does not overwhelm the world. The judgment of God's enemies is postponed. The kingdom that arrived with Jesus did not include the triumphal victory so longed for by the Jews. It arrived secretly like leaven, inconspicuously like a mustard seed, or like a small pearl of great value that can be hidden in one's pocket (Matt. 13:31–46).

The Jewish people expected the kingdom of God to bring the present evil age to an end. But it arrived mysteriously without doing so. The new reality of the kingdom overlapped the present age, invading it rather than bringing it to an end. The demons reflect this oddity when they ask Jesus, "Have you come here to torment us before the time?" (Matt. 8:29). The future kingdom will bring the present age to an end and usher in the perfect age promised in the prophets. The present kingdom is both an anticipation and a guarantee of this future bliss.

The expression "kingdom of God" occurs mostly in the gospels of Matthew, Mark, and Luke. The Gospel of John and the epistles of the New Testament refer to the same reality but in different language, using phrases such as "eternal life" or "salvation." The apostle Paul identified the kingdom of God as "righteousness and peace and joy in the Holy Spirit" (Rom. 14:17). Perhaps one reason why he described it this way is that the kingdom of God was a Jewish expression unfamiliar and possibly misleading to Gentiles.

Some interpreters of the Bible have described the phrase "kingdom of God" as a more comprehensive term referring to both heaven and earth. Likewise, they believe "kingdom of God" is a more restricted term referring to God's rule on earth, especially in relation to the nation of Israel. In this view Jesus offered the literal kingdom of heaven to Israel, but the Jews refused to accept it. Thus, it has been postponed until the Second Coming of Christ.

A careful study of the gospels, however, shows that the two phrases are used interchangeably. In parallel passages, Matthew uses "kingdom of heaven" while Mark and Luke have "kingdom of God" (Matt. 4:17; Mark 1:15). Even in Matthew the two phrases are sometimes used interchangeably, as in Matthew 19:23–24, where they are used one after the other in the same connection.

~Nelson's New Illustrated Bible Dictionary[17]

• List three practical things you could either stop doing or start doing to reflect your belief that Jesus has made you a member of his now-and-not-yet kingdom.

_____

_____

_____

_____

_____

_____

_____

_____

_____

_____

_____

_____

_____

_____

_____

_____

_____

_____

_____

_____

_____

_____

_____

_____

_____

_____

_____

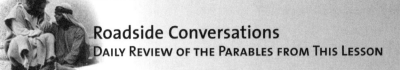

Roadside Conversations
DAILY REVIEW OF THE PARABLES FROM THIS LESSON

Daily Roadside Conversation 1
Canceling the Debt

READ: Matthew 18:23–35
Reflect on this key question:
If sin is like a debt, then forgiveness is like . . . what?

_____

_____

_____

_____

_____

_____

_____

_____

_____

_____

_____

_____

_____

_____

Resolve to be a person who freely shares with others the forgiveness that God has given to you.

Suggested prayer: Lord, keep me from being a person who harbors grudges or who pleads for your mercy and then refuses to be merciful to others. Give me the grace to know how to forgive. Amen.

Daily Roadside Conversation 2
Just Do It!

READ: Matthew 21:28–32
Reflect on this key question:
What are some ways I act like I plan to obey God, but I never seem to get around to doing what he wants?

_____

_____

_____

_____

_____

_____

_____

_____

_____

_____

_____

_____

Resolve to be a person whose only response to the revealed will of God is "Yes, Lord."

Suggested prayer: God, forgive me for the times I defy you. Forgive me for the times I lie to you–saying I'm going to do something and then not keeping my word. Make me a true servant who does what you say–no matter how difficult. Amen.

Daily Roadside Conversation 3
Hardheartedness

READ: Matthew 21:33–45

Reflect on this key question:

How could the Pharisees and religious leaders have had such close exposure to Jesus—hearing him teach and seeing him do miracles right before their eyes—and still have been so stubbornly opposed to him?

_____
_____
_____
_____
_____
_____
_____
_____
_____
_____
_____
_____
_____
_____

Resolve to let Jesus surprise you—and to trust him even when he doesn't meet your expectations.

Suggested prayer: Lord Jesus, please keep me from the kind of pride that would scoff at your words, ignore them, and treat you with contempt or disrespect. May your will–not mine–be done on earth, and in my life, as it is in heaven. Amen.

Daily Roadside Conversation 4
RSVP

READ: Matthew 22:2–14

Reflect on this key question:

What specific role can I play in inviting people to come experience the joy of God's kingdom?

_____
_____
_____
_____
_____
_____
_____
_____
_____
_____
_____
_____
_____
_____

Resolve to be like God in this way: continuing to extend the invitation of grace even when people spurn God's offer of eternal life.

Suggested prayer: Father, you have been so gracious to me. Thank you for showing me the truth of your love. I know there will be many who reject your offer of forgiveness and life, but that doesn't absolve me of my responsibility to keep announcing this Good News to all who will listen. Give me opportunities—today!—to witness for you. Amen.

Daily Roadside Conversation 5
Be Prepared

Read: Matthew 24:32–34; 25:1–13

Reflect on this key question:

If a team of friends and theologians examined my life closely, would they conclude I really believe that Christ is coming back at any moment to establish his kingdom?

_____
_____
_____
_____
_____
_____
_____
_____
_____
_____
_____
_____
_____

Resolve to live out the truth of 1 John 2:28: "And now, little children, abide in Him, that when He appears, we may have confidence and not be ashamed before Him at His coming" (NKJV).

Suggested prayer: Lord, your Word speaks of a future kingdom that will arrive with your return. Let this promise be the great hope of my life. Let me be ever conscious of the truth that your reign is both present and future. Remind me in countless ways every single day to live with that great expectation in view. Amen.

1. John MacArthur, *MacArthur Bible Studies, Mark: The Humanity of Christ* (Nashville: W Publishing, 2000), 25–26.

2. *The Nelson Study Bible,* INDepth note, *Parables: More Than Stories* (Nashville: Thomas Nelson Publishers, 1997), 1613.

3. Peter Wallace, *What Jesus Is Saying to You Today* (Nashville: Thomas Nelson Publishers, 1994), Day 115.

4. John MacArthur, *The MacArthur Study Bible,* introduction to *The Gospel According to Matthew* (Nashville: W Publishing, 1997), 1389.

5. John MacArthur, *The MacArthur Study Bible,* study note (Nashville: W Publishing, 1997), 1396.

6. John MacArthur, *The MacArthur Study Bible,* introduction to *The Gospel According to Matthew* (Nashville: W Publishing, 1997), 1389.

7. Charles Swindoll, *The Grace Awakening* (W Publishing, 1990), 31.

8. Ronald F. Youngblood, General Editor, F. F. Bruce and R. K. Harrison, Consulting Editors, *Nelson's New Illustrated Bible Dictionary* (Nashville: Thomas Nelson Publishers, 1997), 73.

9. Max Anders, *What You Need to Know about Salvation* (Nashville: Thomas Nelson Publishers, 1997), 136–137.

10. Albert M. Wells Jr., *Inspiring Quotations Contemporary and Classical* (Nashville: Thomas Nelson Publishers, 1988), 83.

11. Max Anders, *What You Need to Know about Salvation* (Nashville: Thomas Nelson Publishers, 1997), 78.

12. Ronald F. Youngblood, General Editor, F. F. Bruce and R. K. Harrison, Consulting Editors, *Nelson's New Illustrated Bible Dictionary* (Nashville: Thomas Nelson Publishers, 1997), 1228.

13. *The Nelson Study Bible,* study note, (Nashville: Thomas Nelson Publishers, 1997), 1598–99.

14. W. A. Criswell, *Believers Study Bible* [electronic edition] (Nashville: Thomas Nelson Publishers, 1997).

15. Ronald F. Youngblood, General Editor, F. F. Bruce and R. K. Harrison, Consulting Editors, *Nelson's New Illustrated Bible Dictionary* (Nashville: Thomas Nelson Publishers, 1997), 1116.

16. Albert M. Wells, Jr., *Inspiring Quotations Contemporary and Classical* (Nashville: Thomas Nelson Publishers, 1988), 92–93.

17. Ronald F. Youngblood, General Editor, F. F. Bruce and R. K. Harrison, Consulting Editors, *Nelson's New Illustrated Bible Dictionary* (Nashville: Thomas Nelson Publishers, 1997), 729–731.